FOR EACH SWEET

A joyful story that helps children discover
the sweetness of real food

Jean A. Gibson

Hermanstyne Press

For information contact: jgibs60@yahoo.com

Written by J.A Gibson

Illustrated by Sourav Majumder

Edited by Amy Betz, formerly of Scholastic

ISBN: 978-0-9979662-2-0

Published by Hermanstyne Press

Printed in the United States of America

Dedication:

To my first grandson, Christofer Armaan Aarons

You are my inspiration

Thank you for choosing me

BAKERY

For each ice cream scoop
You can bloat like a baloon
ICE CREAM
ICE CREAM

FROZEN YOGURT

Frozen Yogurt - yum!

For each piece of gum
You feel hungry, then eat more

Fruit - the better choice

For each slice of cake
Your belly fat can increase

Nuts, seeds - quite a treat

For each soda pop
You put bubbles in your gut

Fruit juice - delicious!

CHOCOLATE

For each chocolate bar
You're on a roller coaster

How about popcorn!

LEMON
GRAPE
CHERRY
ZOO

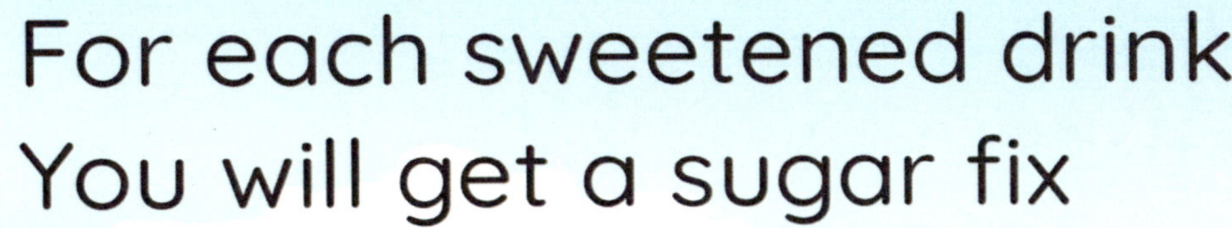

For each sweetened drink
You will get a sugar fix

Water - essential

For each sweet you eat
Eat less and ... ...

.... choose good food groups
To improve your health

For each sweet you eat

Choose the sweetness of real food

For a healthy life

Author's Note

Jean Gibson, a medical practitioner and educator has spent over 25 years advocating for health and wellness. She believes that children learn best when they are given the correct information at an early age, delivered with pattern and rhythm.

For Each Sweet was written in a playful, empowering way to help children discover alternative sweets that are healthy - nature's choice.

When Jean is not devoting her time to healthcare, she enjoys curating projects and living her best life.

FOR EACH SWEET

For each ice cream scoop
You can bloat like a balloon
Frozen Yogurt - yum

For each piece of gum
You feel hungry, then eat more
Fruit - the better choice

For each slice of cake
Your belly fat can increase
Nuts, seeds - quite a treat

For each soda pop
You put bubbles in your gut
Fruit juice - delicious!

For each chocolate bar
You're on a roller coaster
How about popcorn!

For each sweetened drink
You will get a sugar fix
Water - essential

For each sweet you eat
Eat less and choose good food groups
To improve your health

Jean A. Gibson

Hermanstyne Press

* 9 7 8 0 9 9 9 7 9 6 6 2 2 0 *